Mandalas Coloring Book For Relaxation
Stress Less Coloring

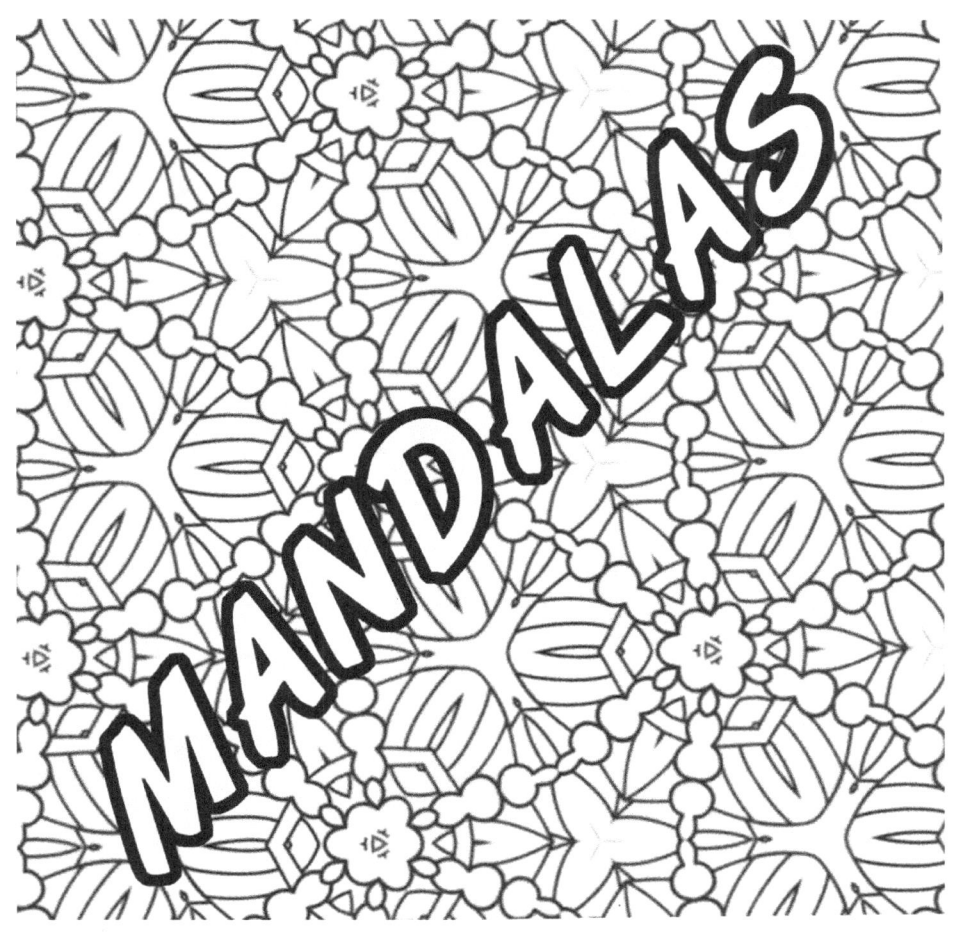

Jasmine Andrews

Mandalas Coloring Book For Relaxation Stress Less Coloring

Copyright: Published in the United States by Jasmine Andrews
Published January 2017

ISBN-13: 978-1542758192

ISBN-10: 154275819X

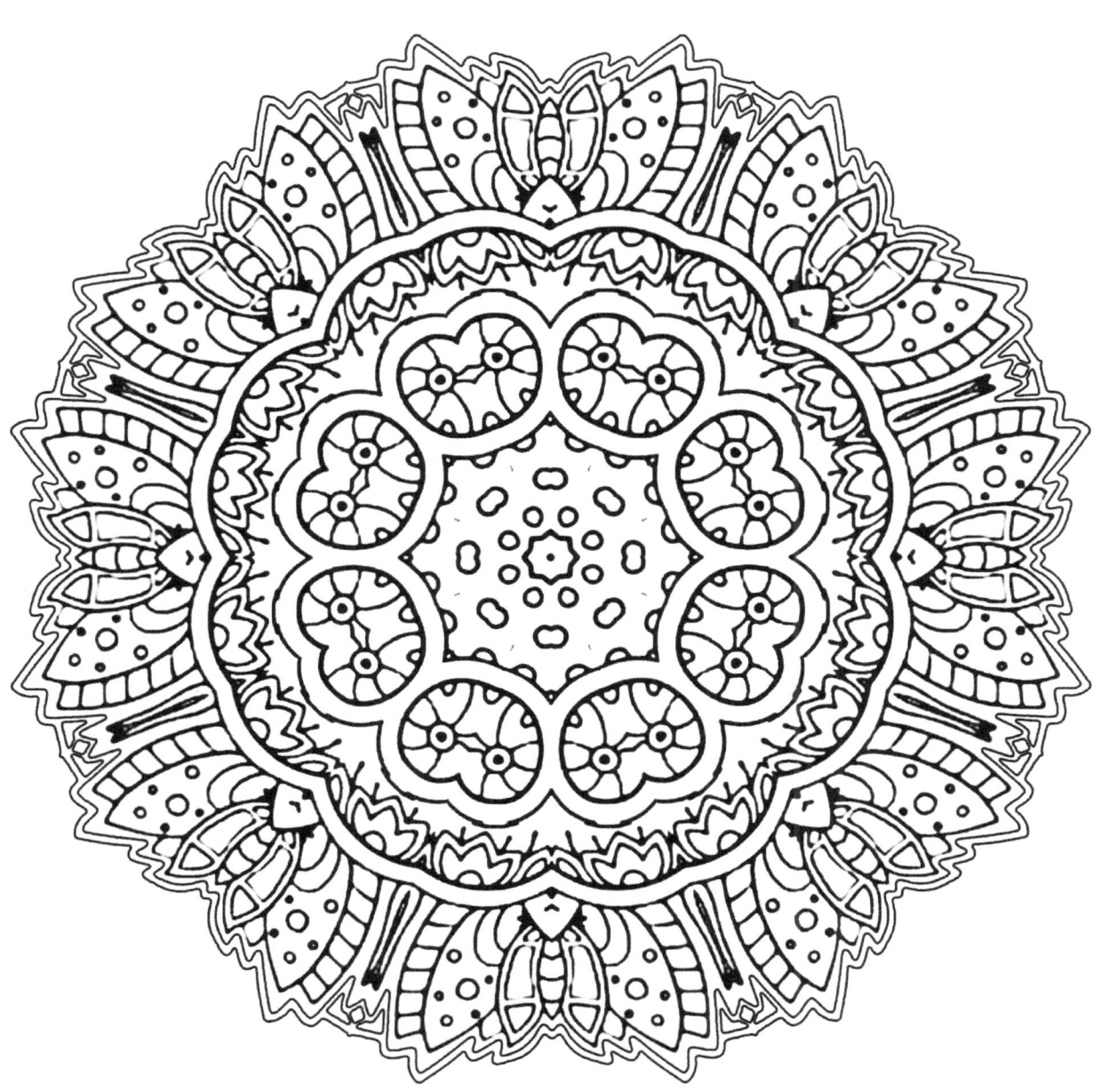

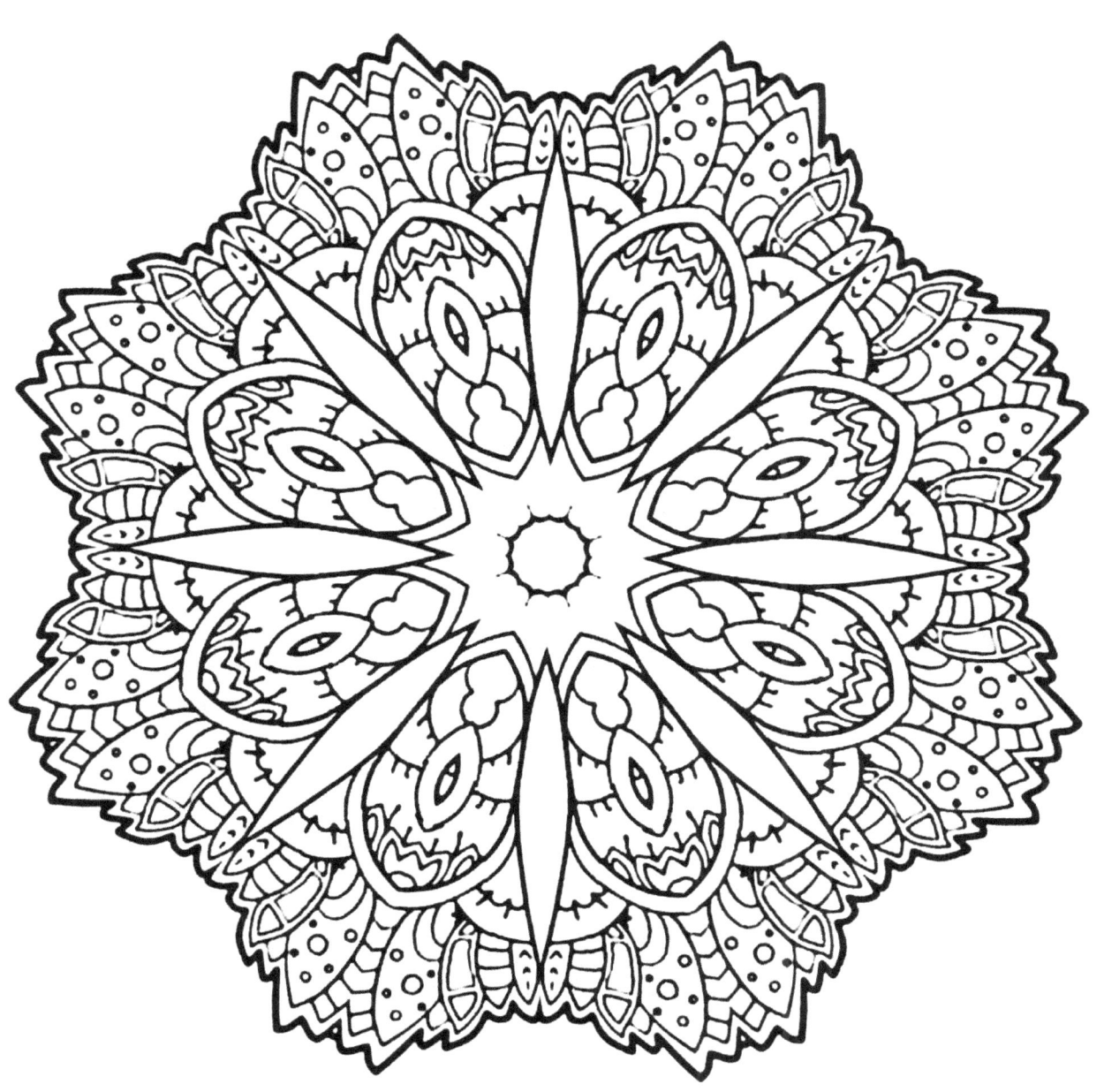

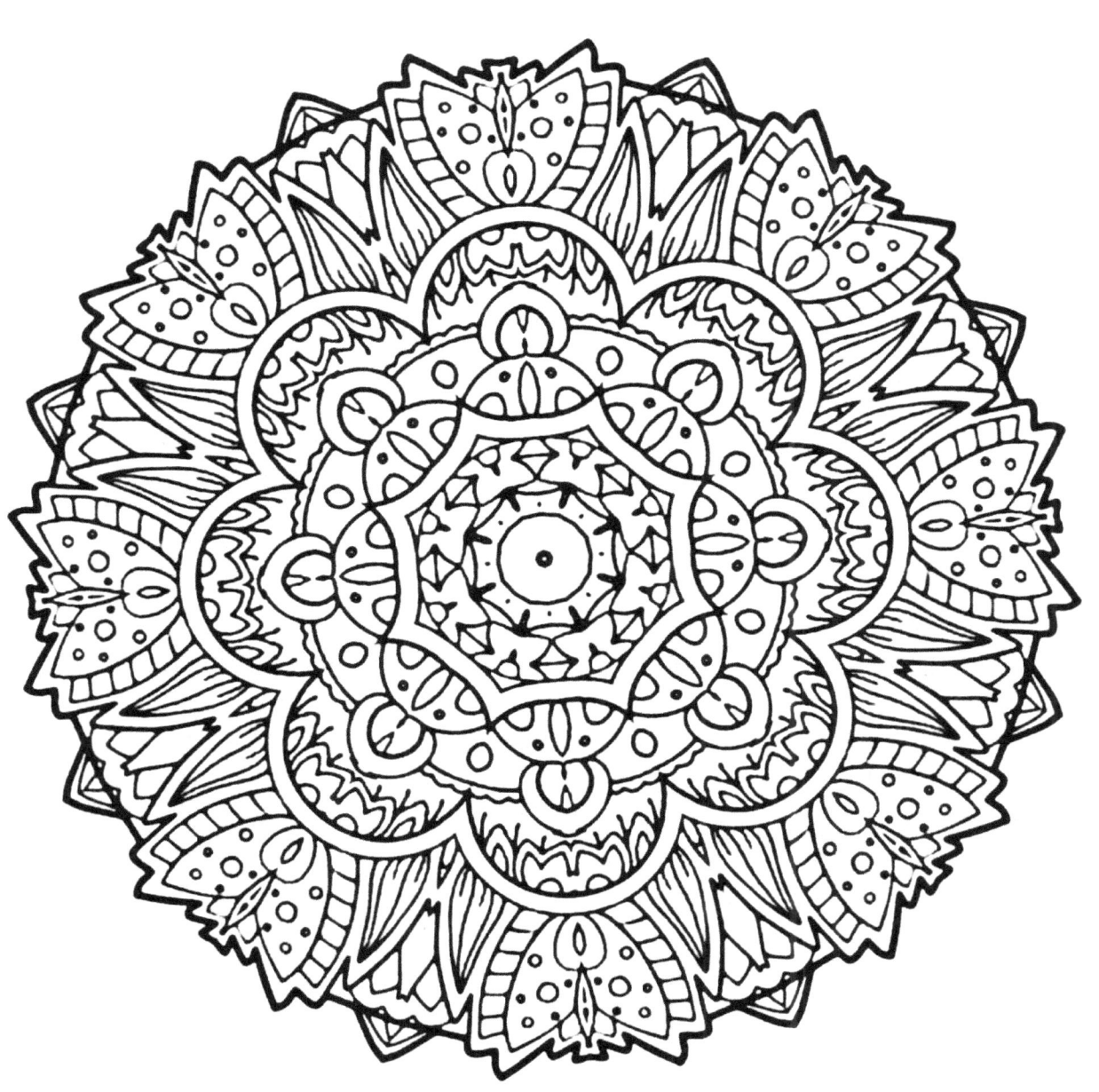

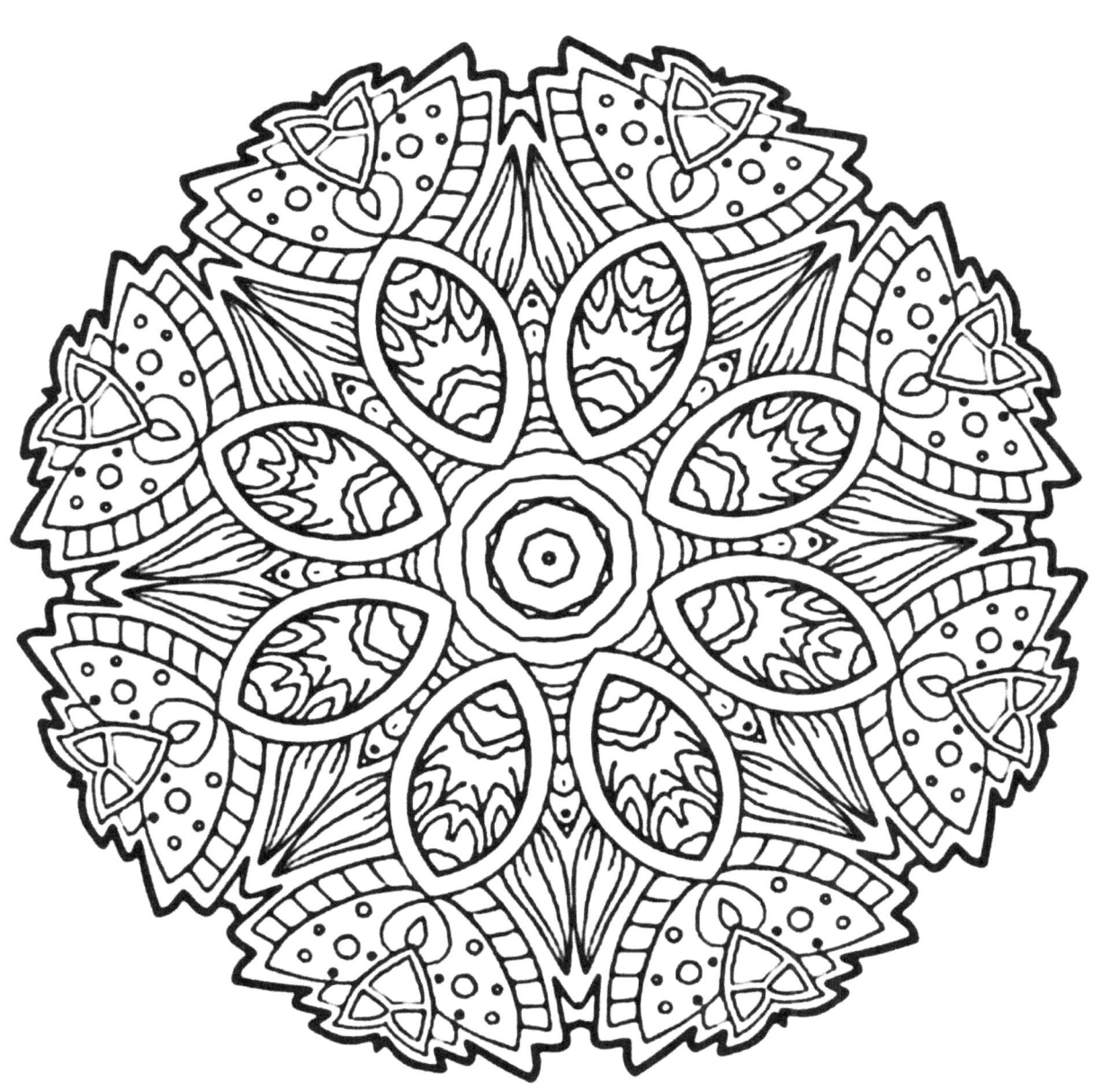

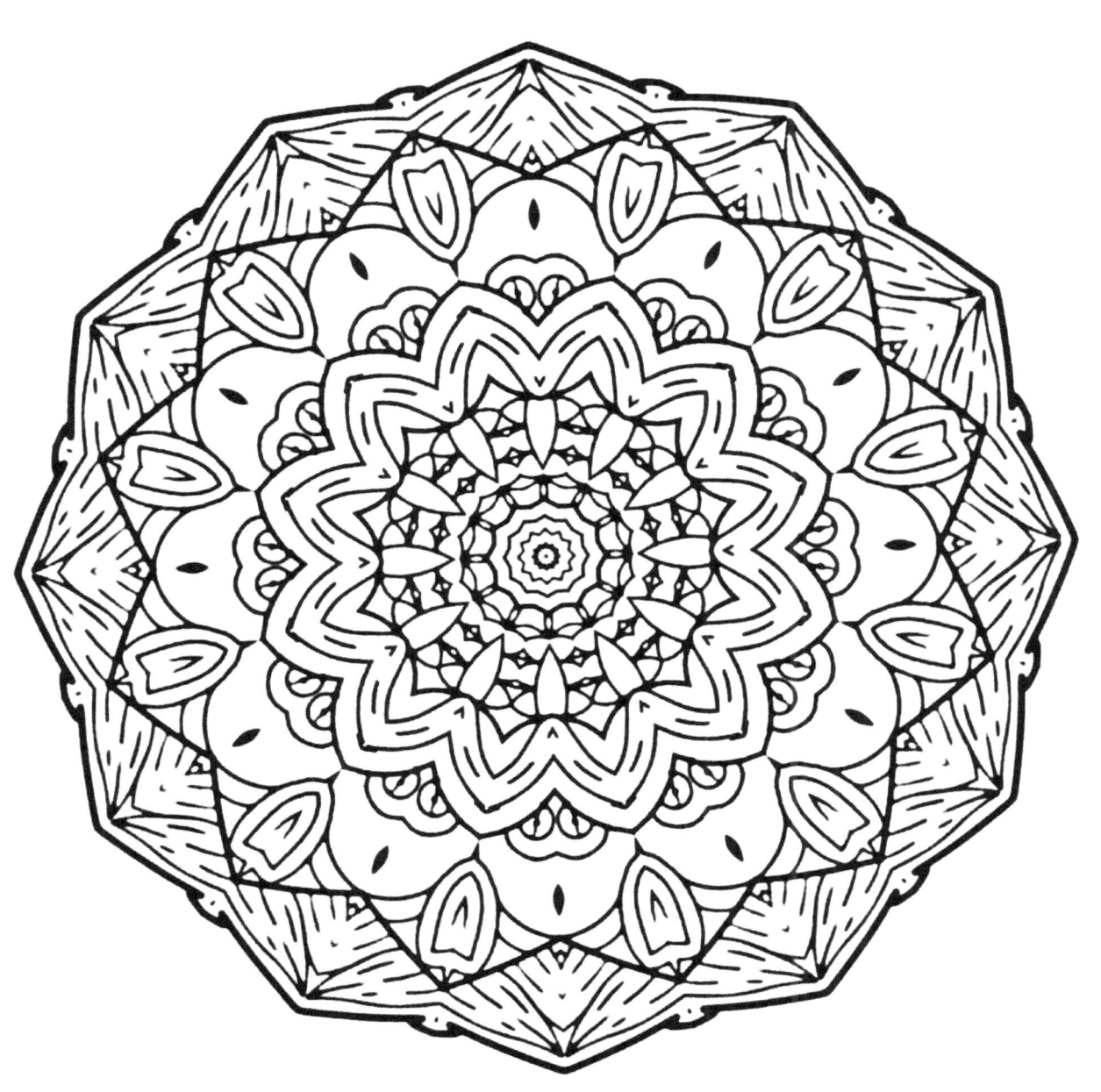

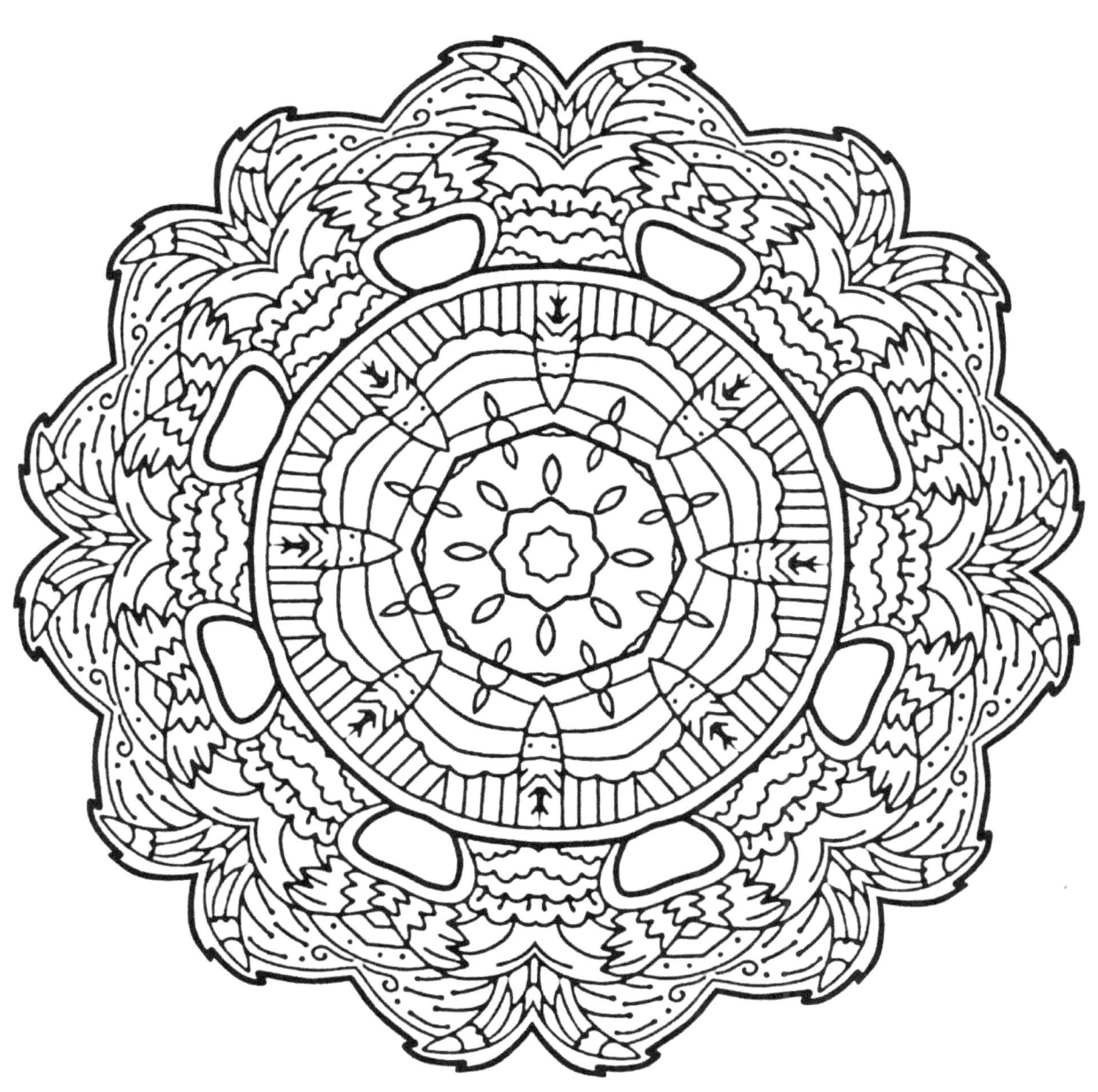

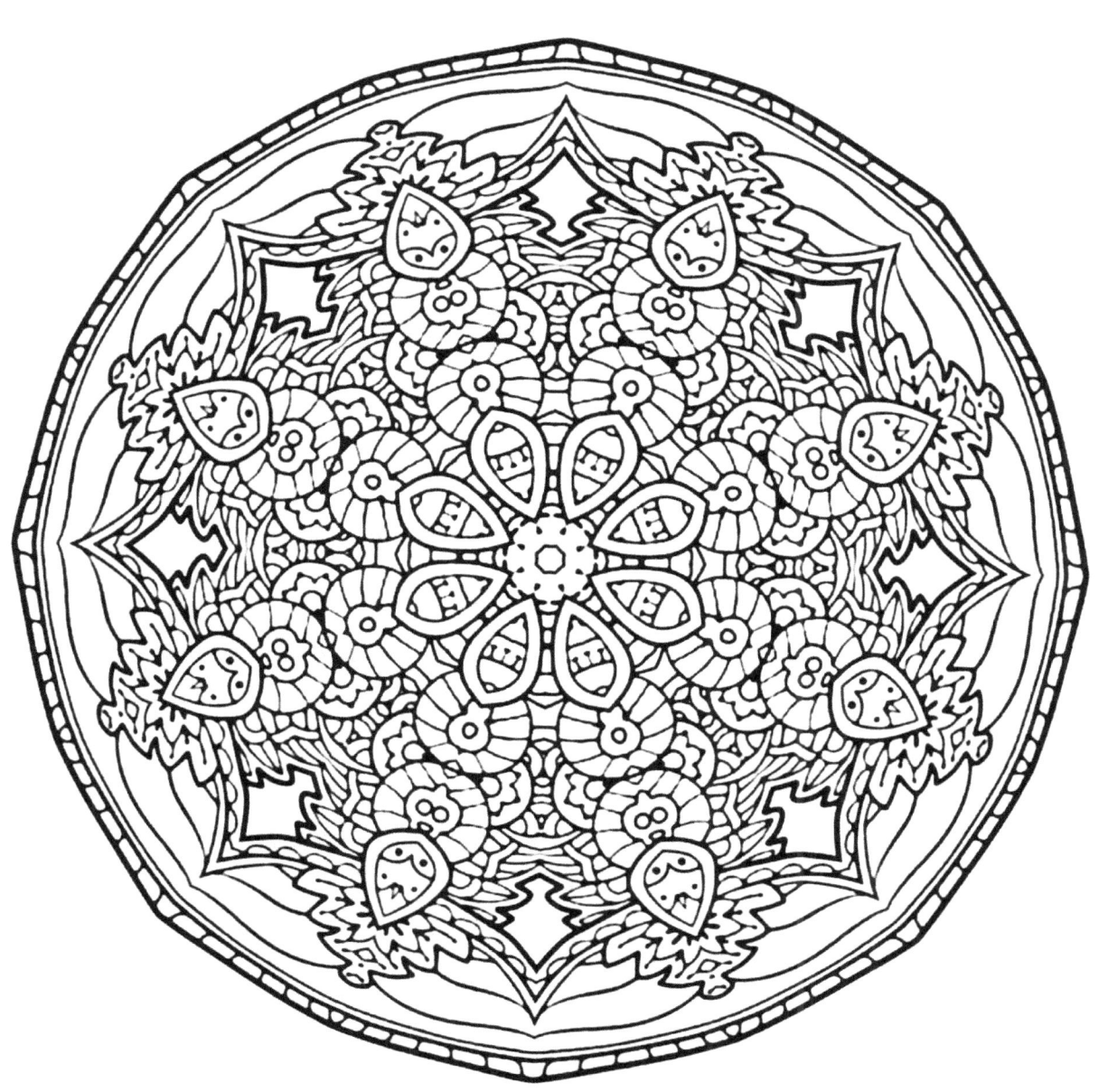

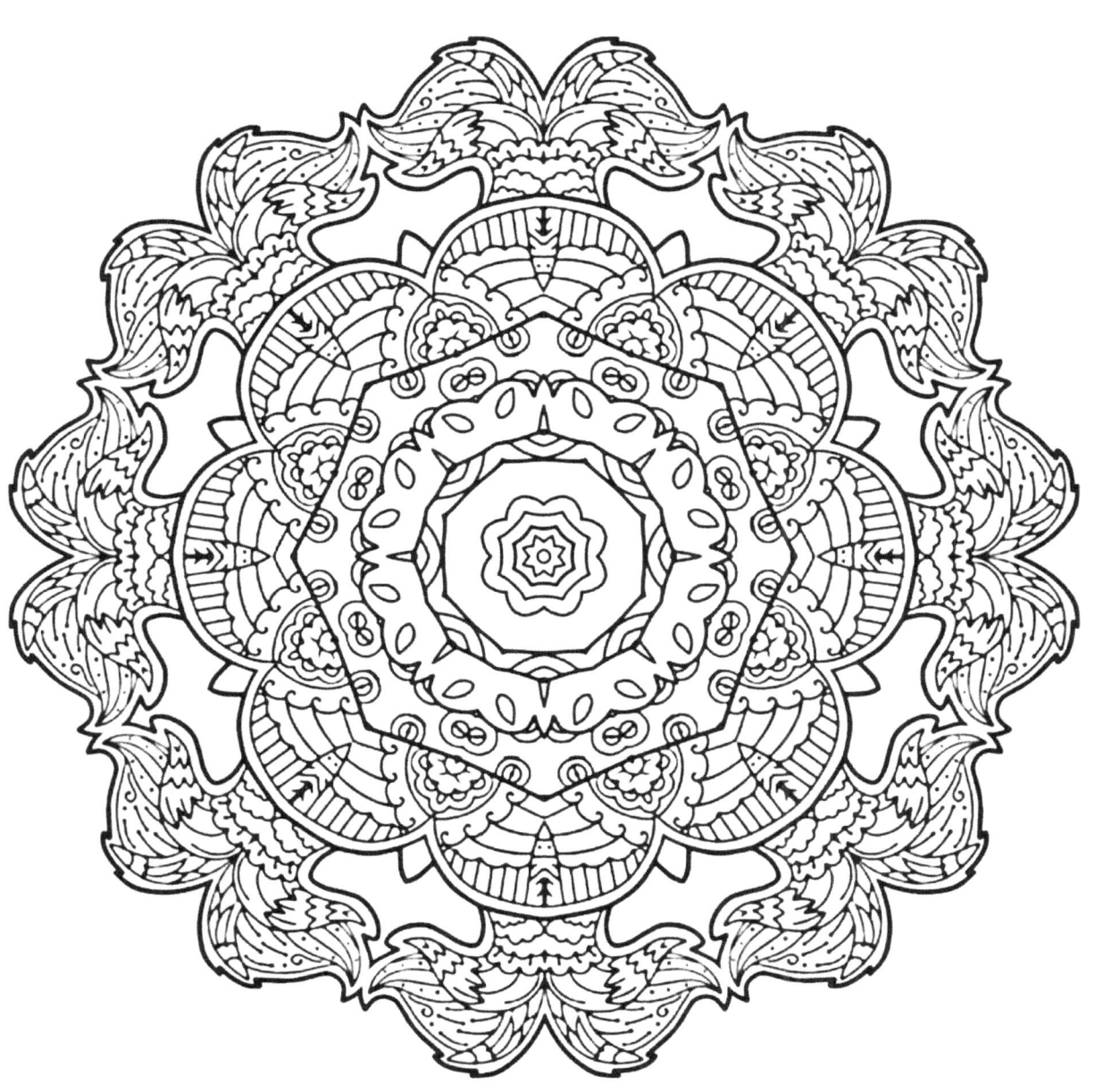

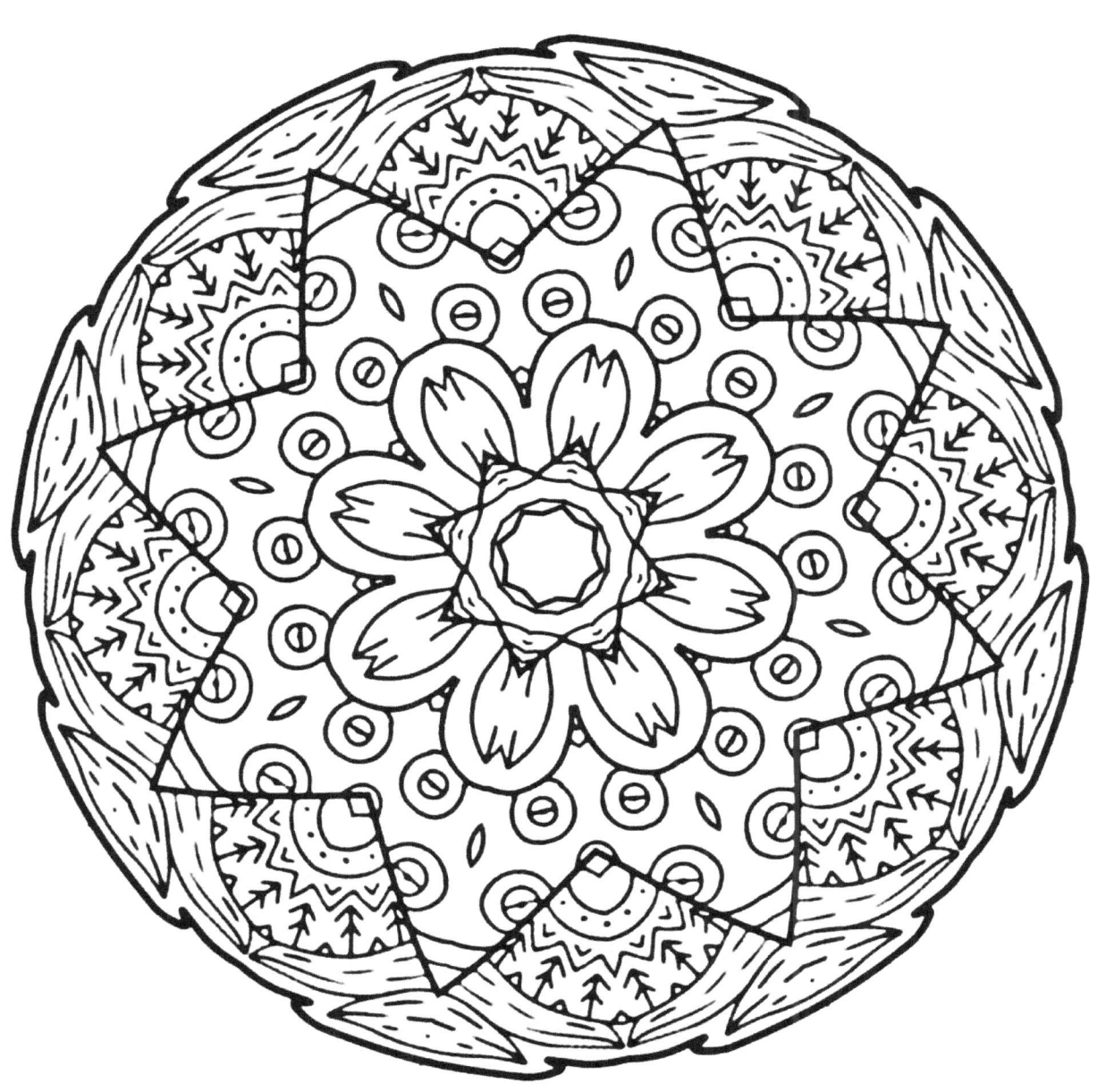

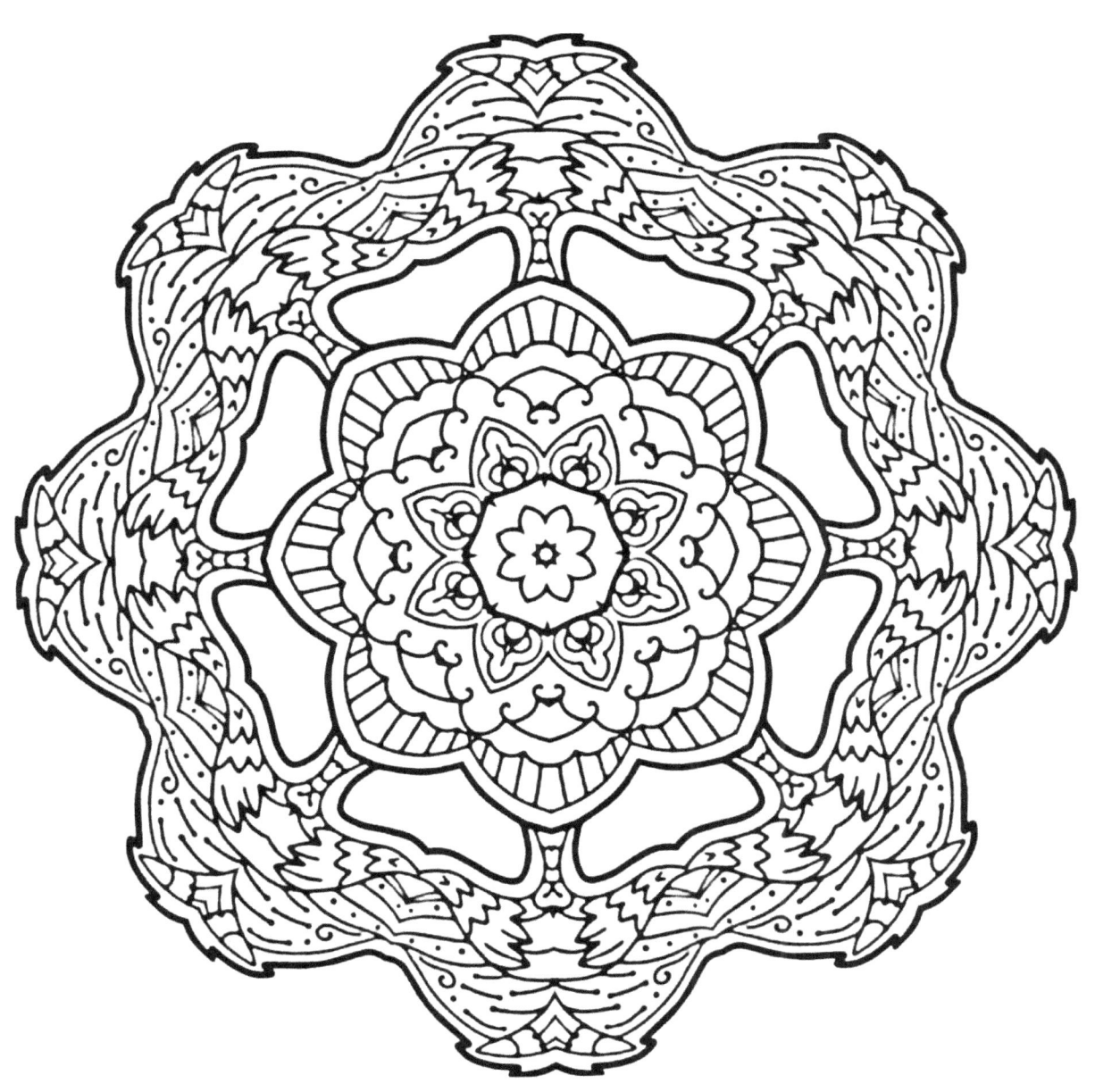

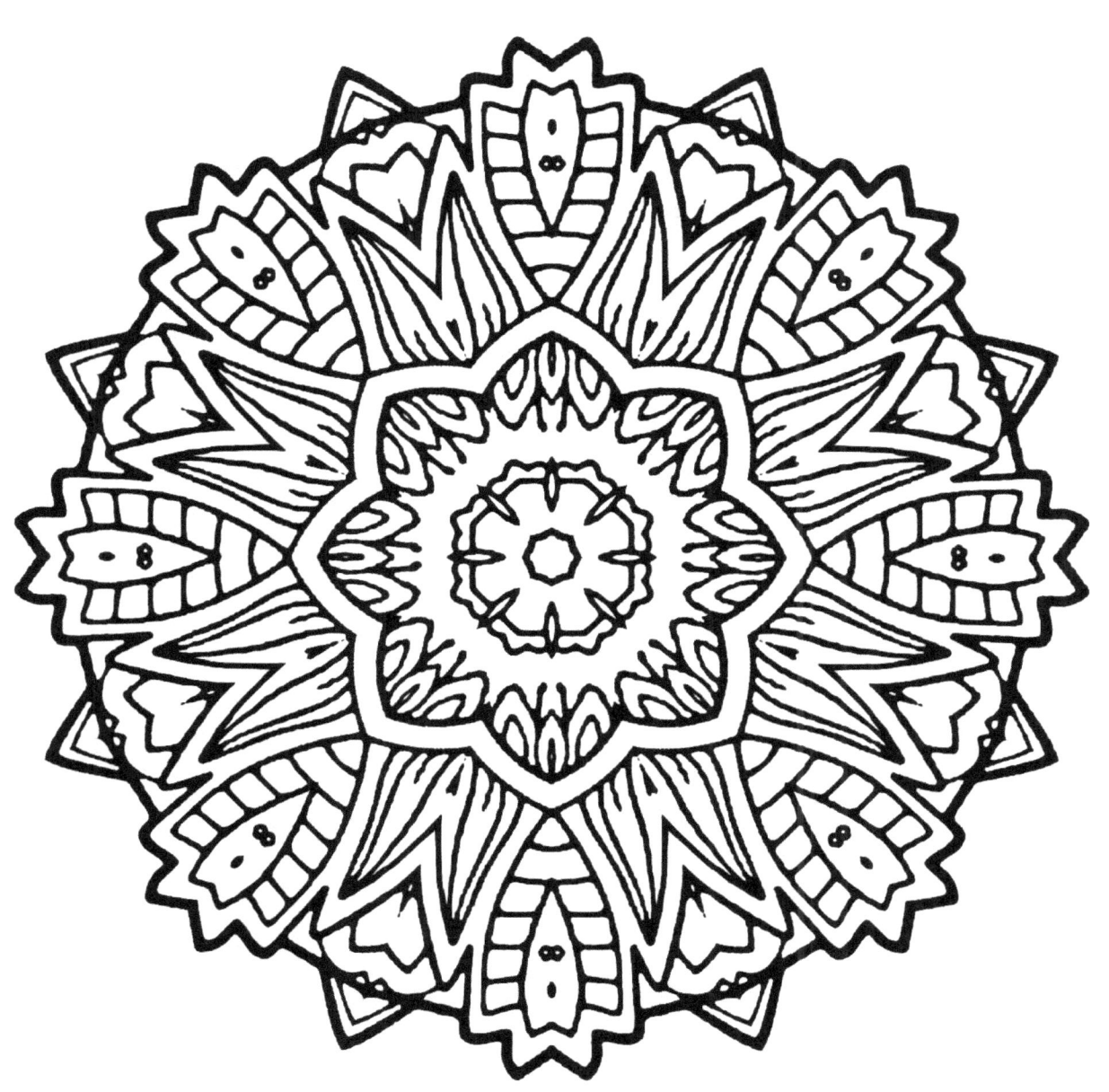

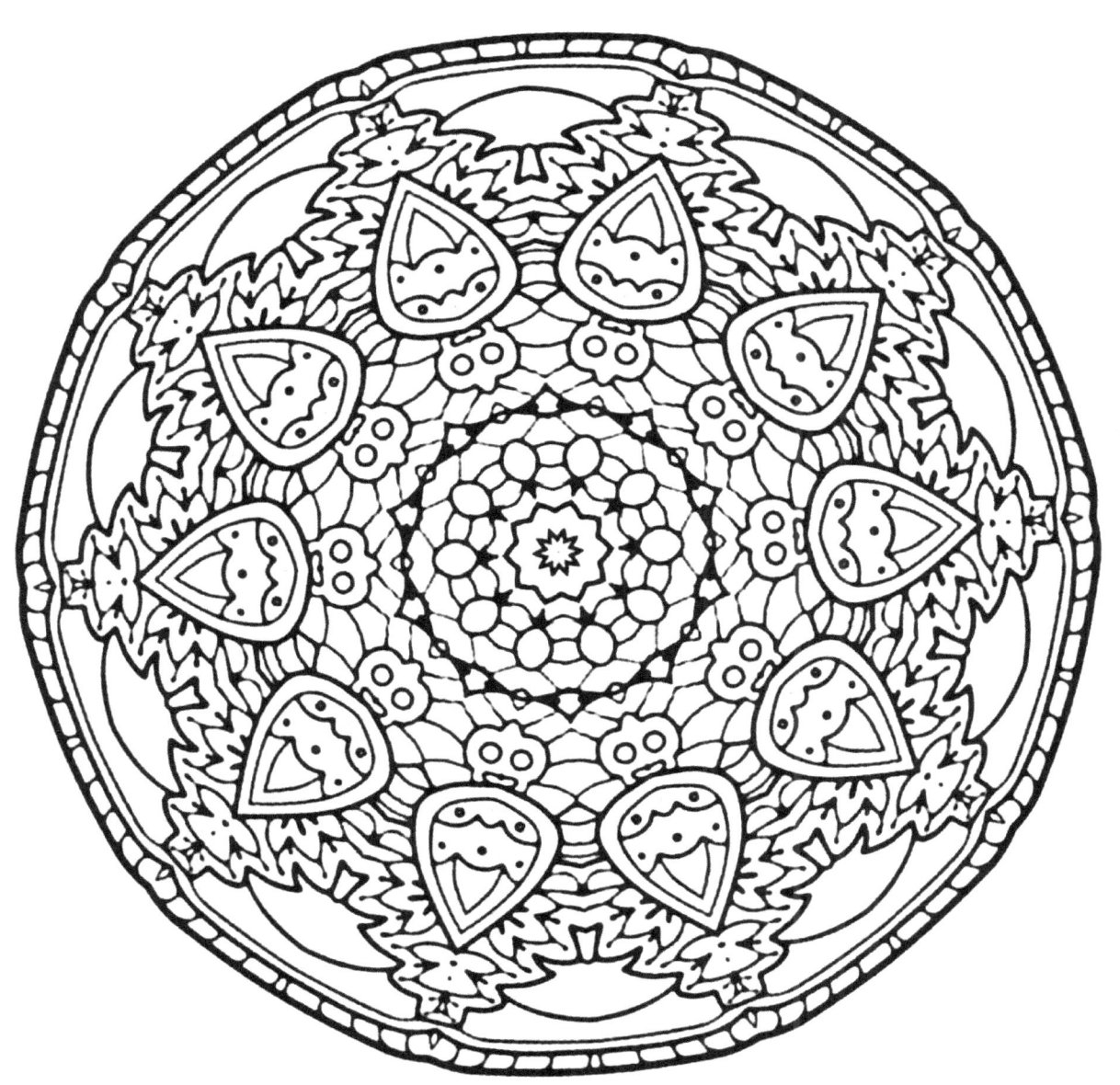

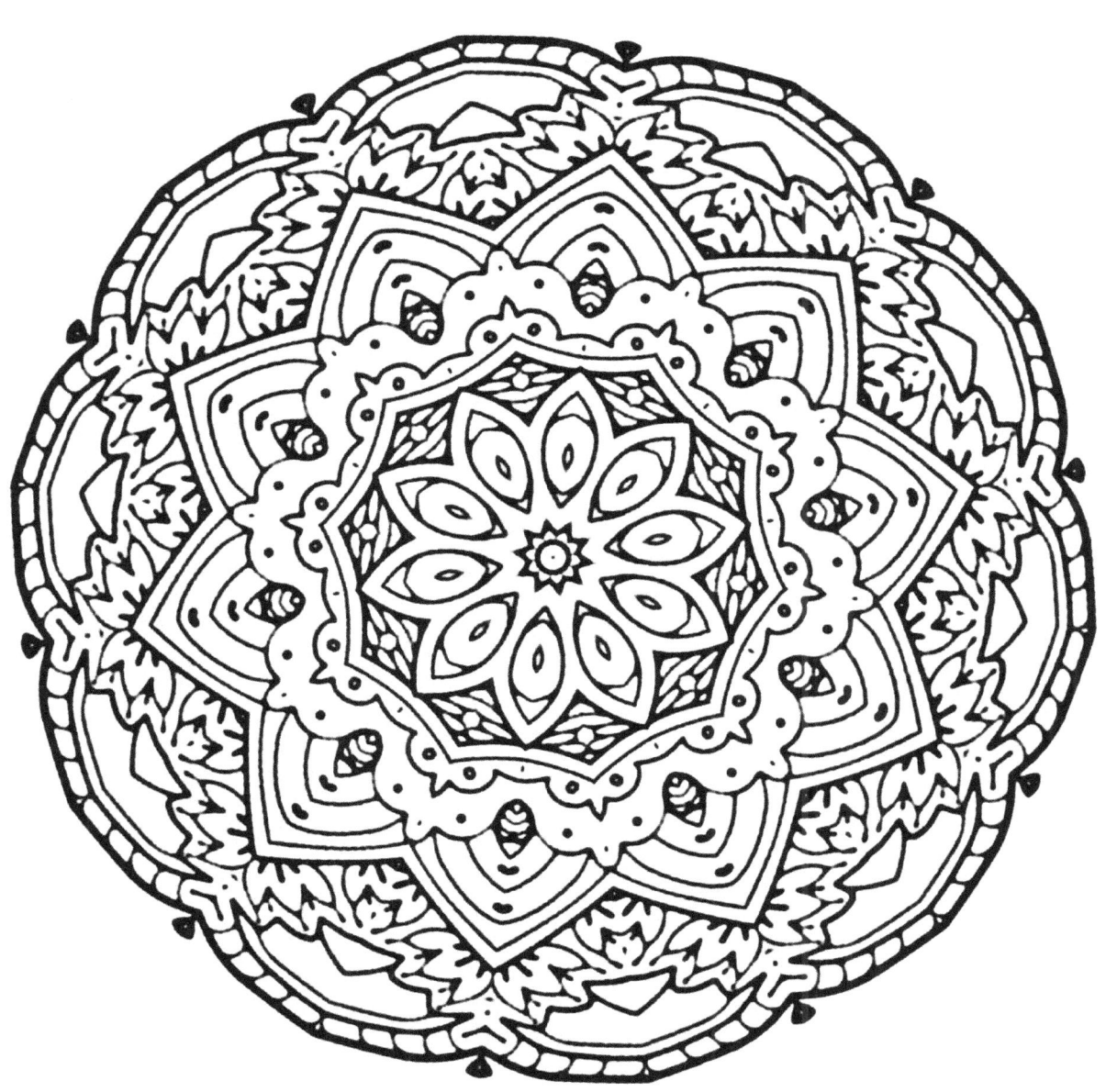

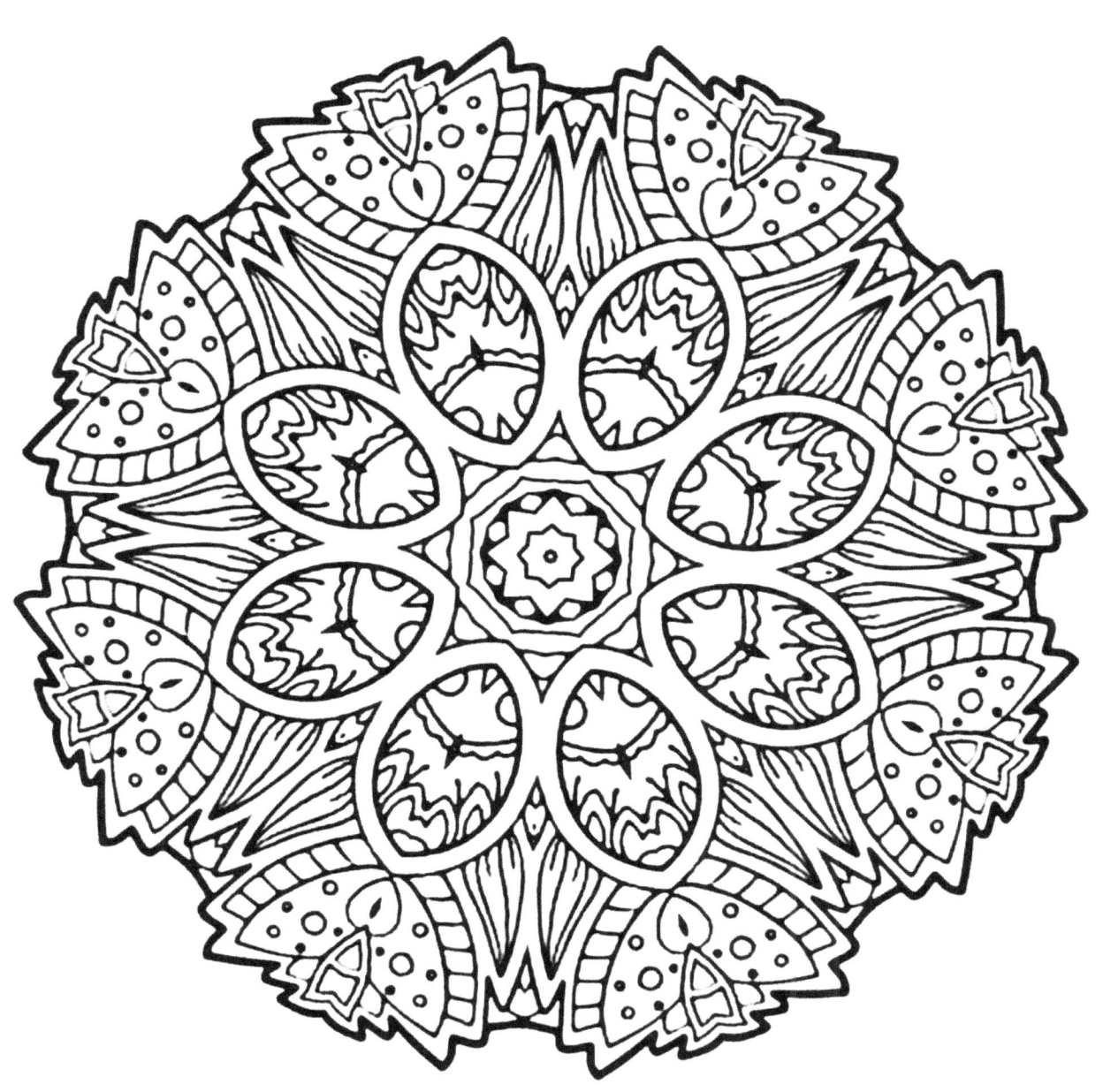

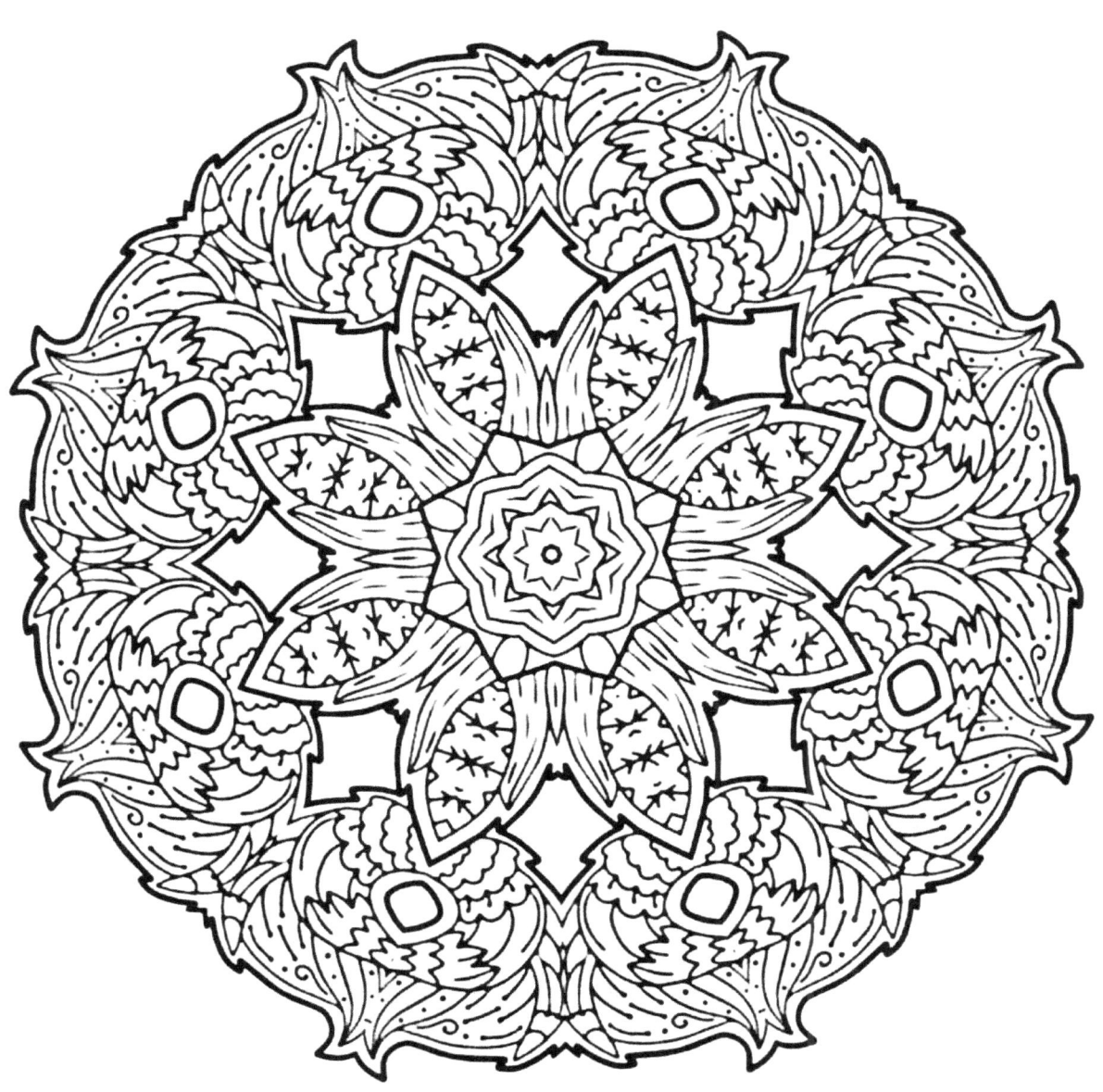

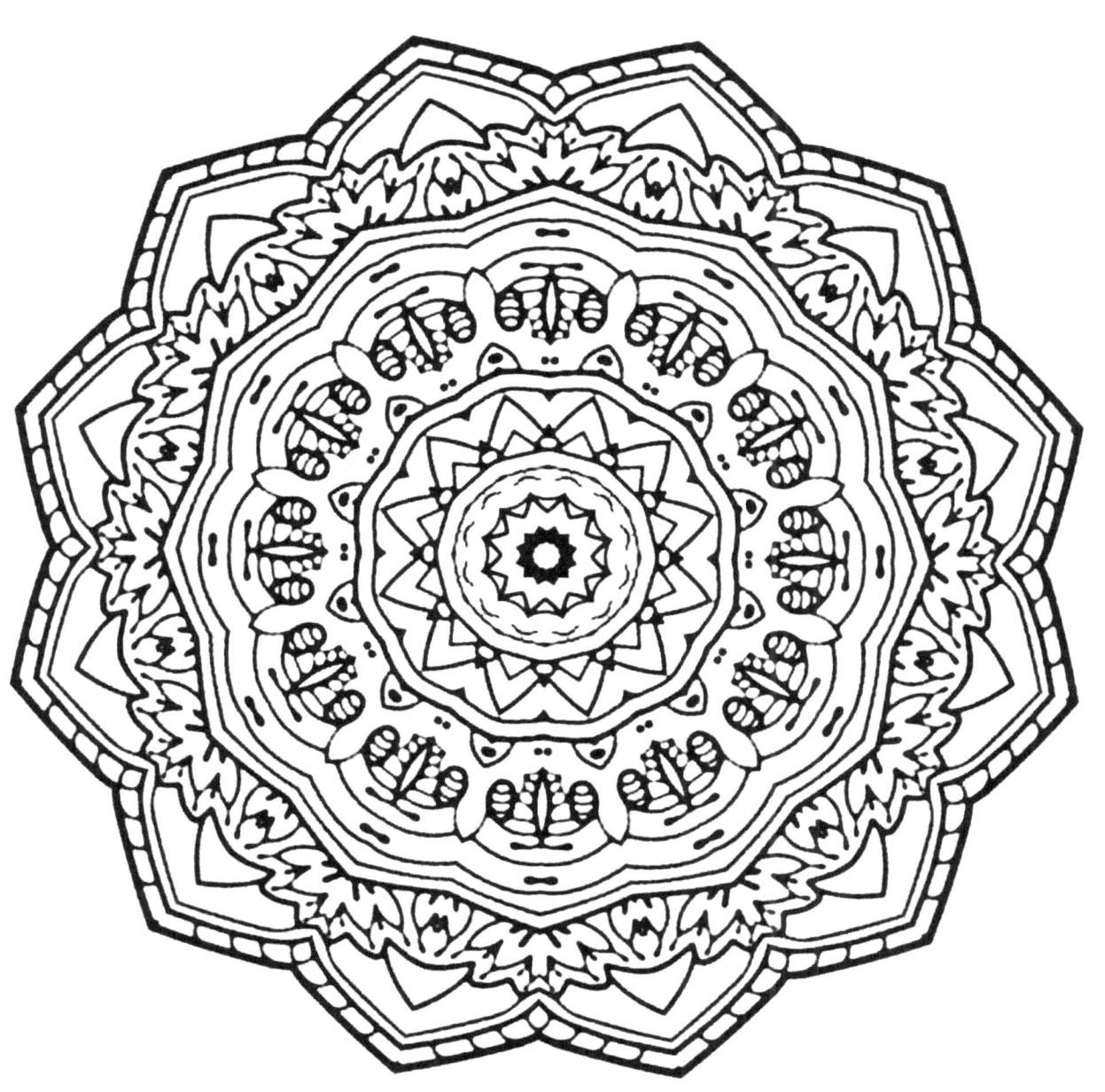

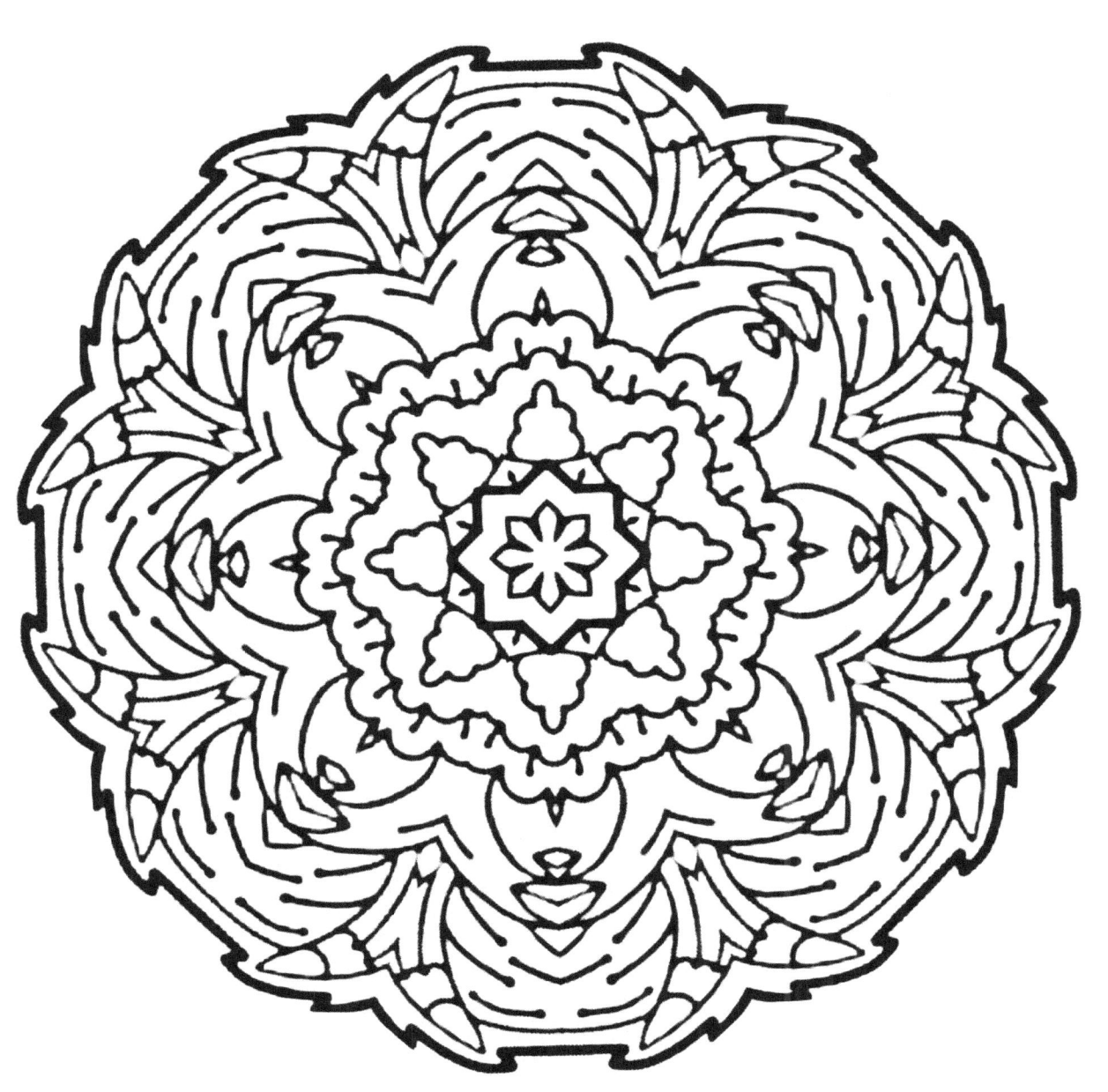

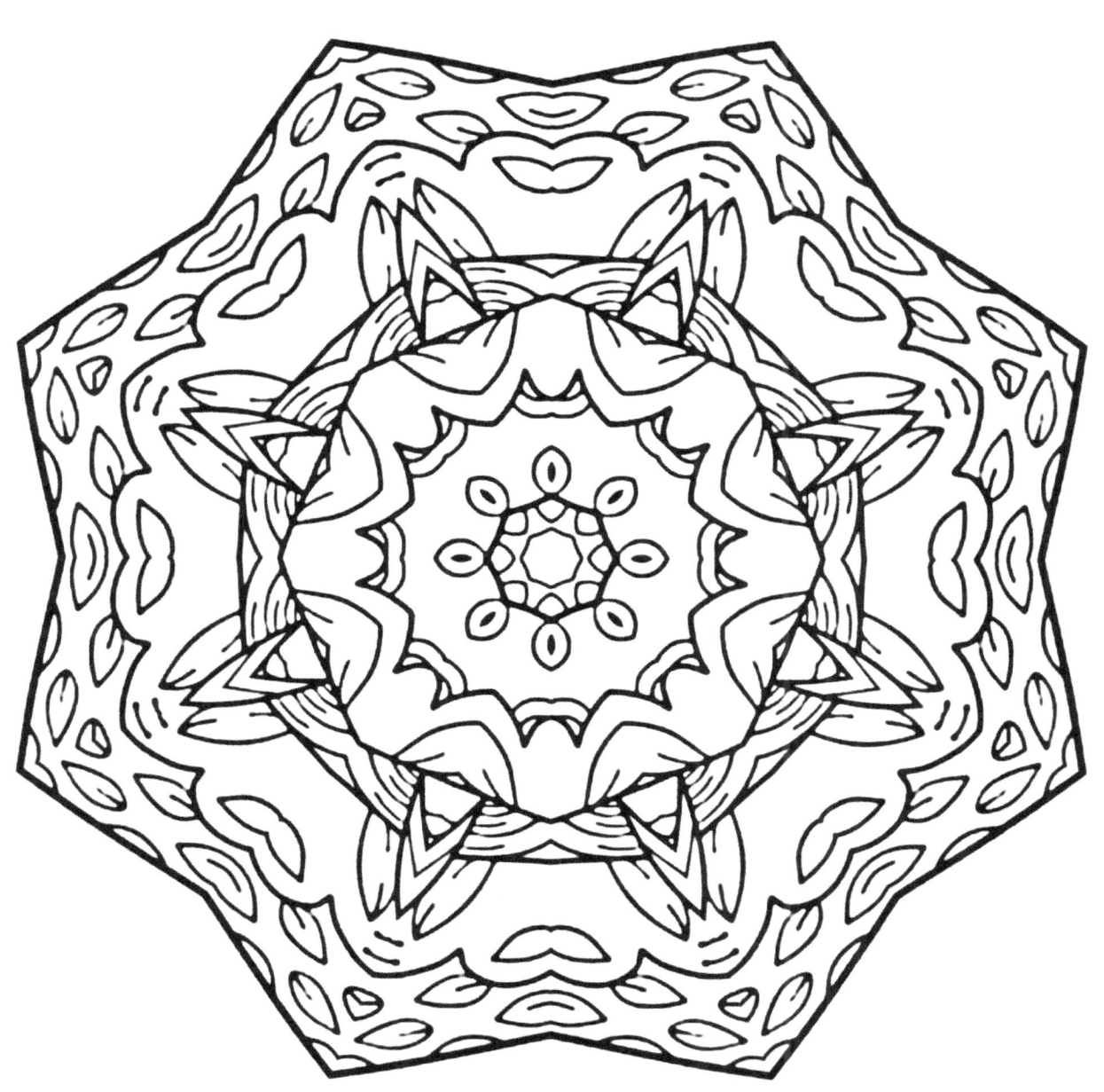

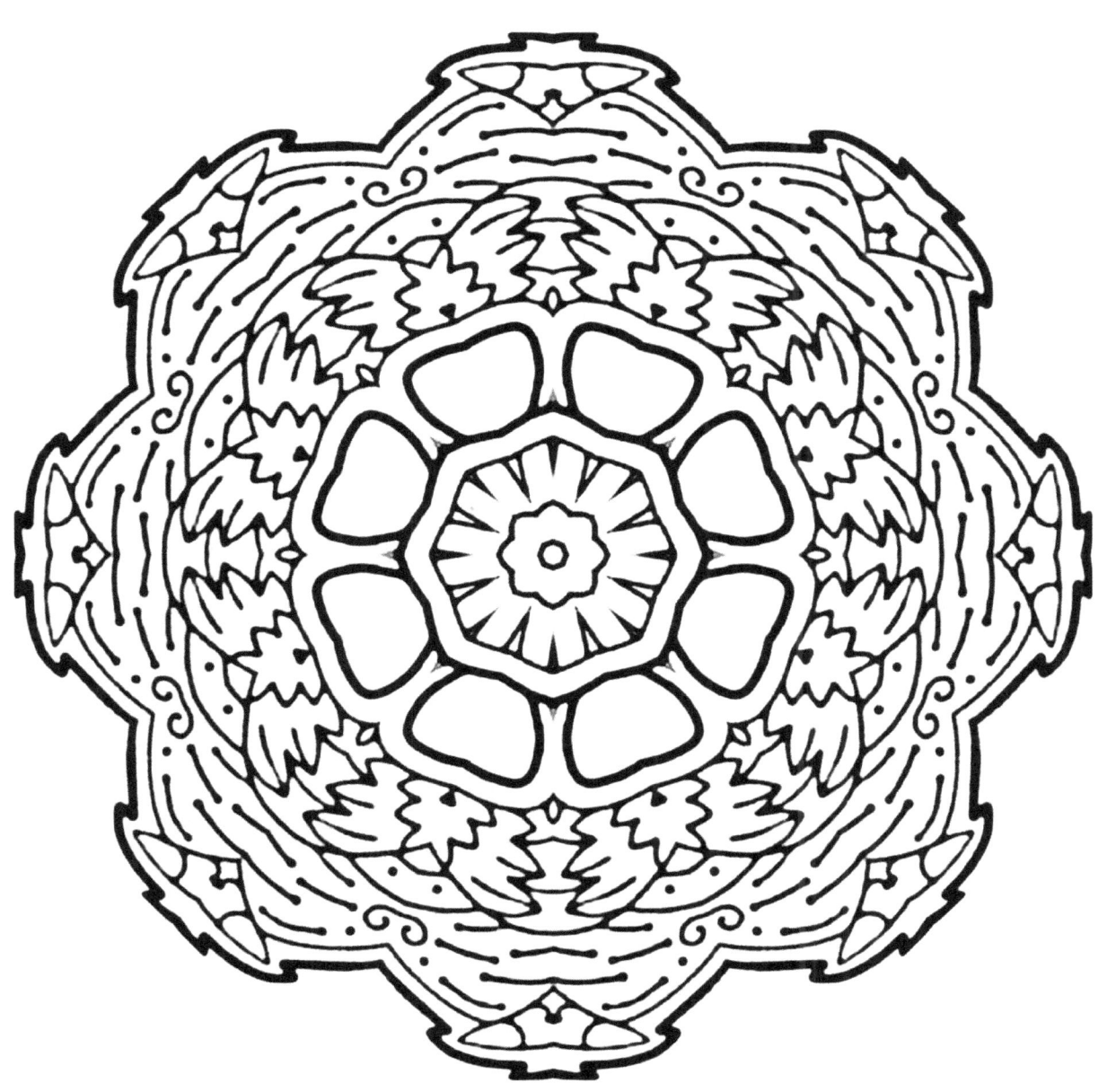

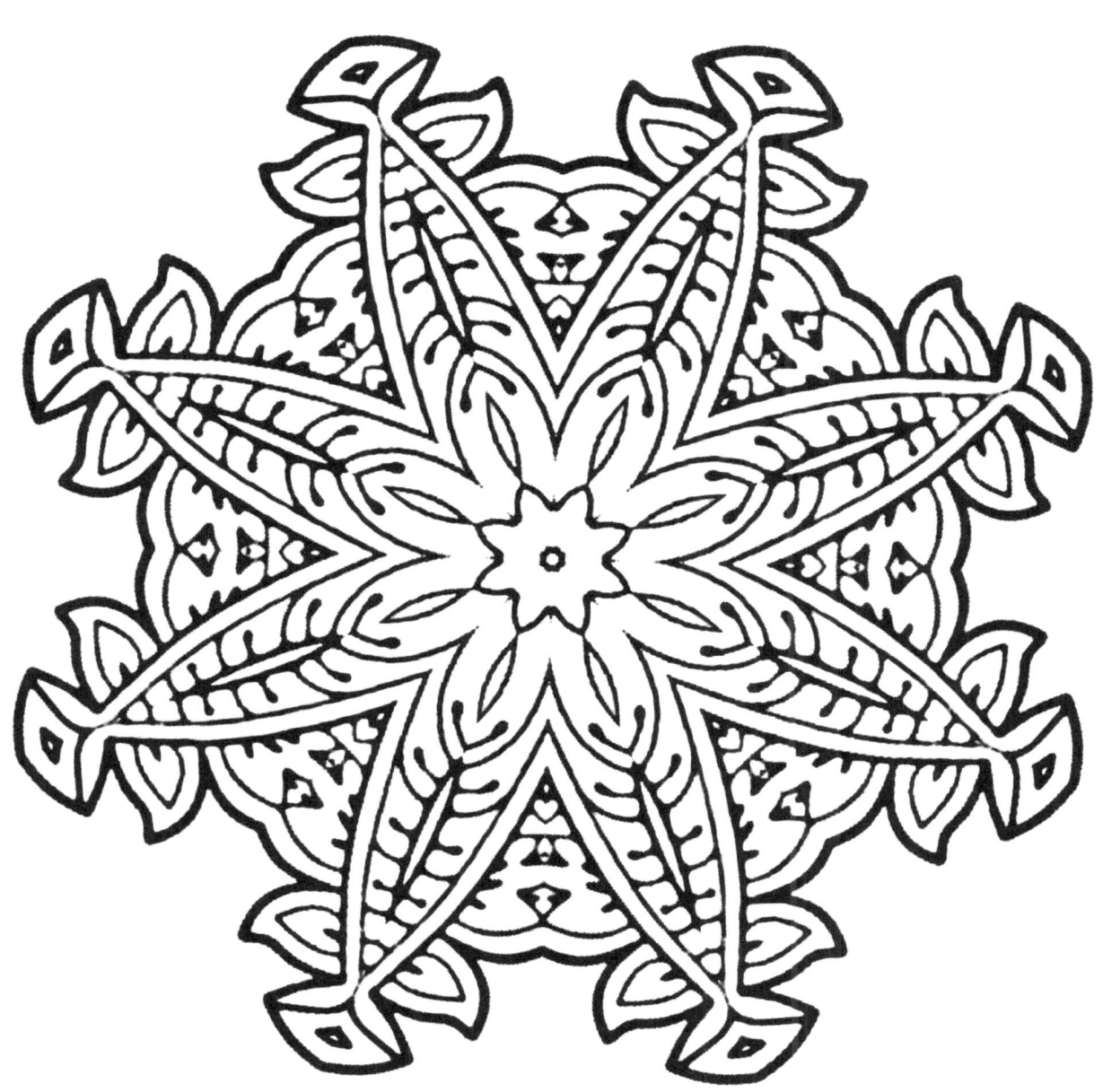

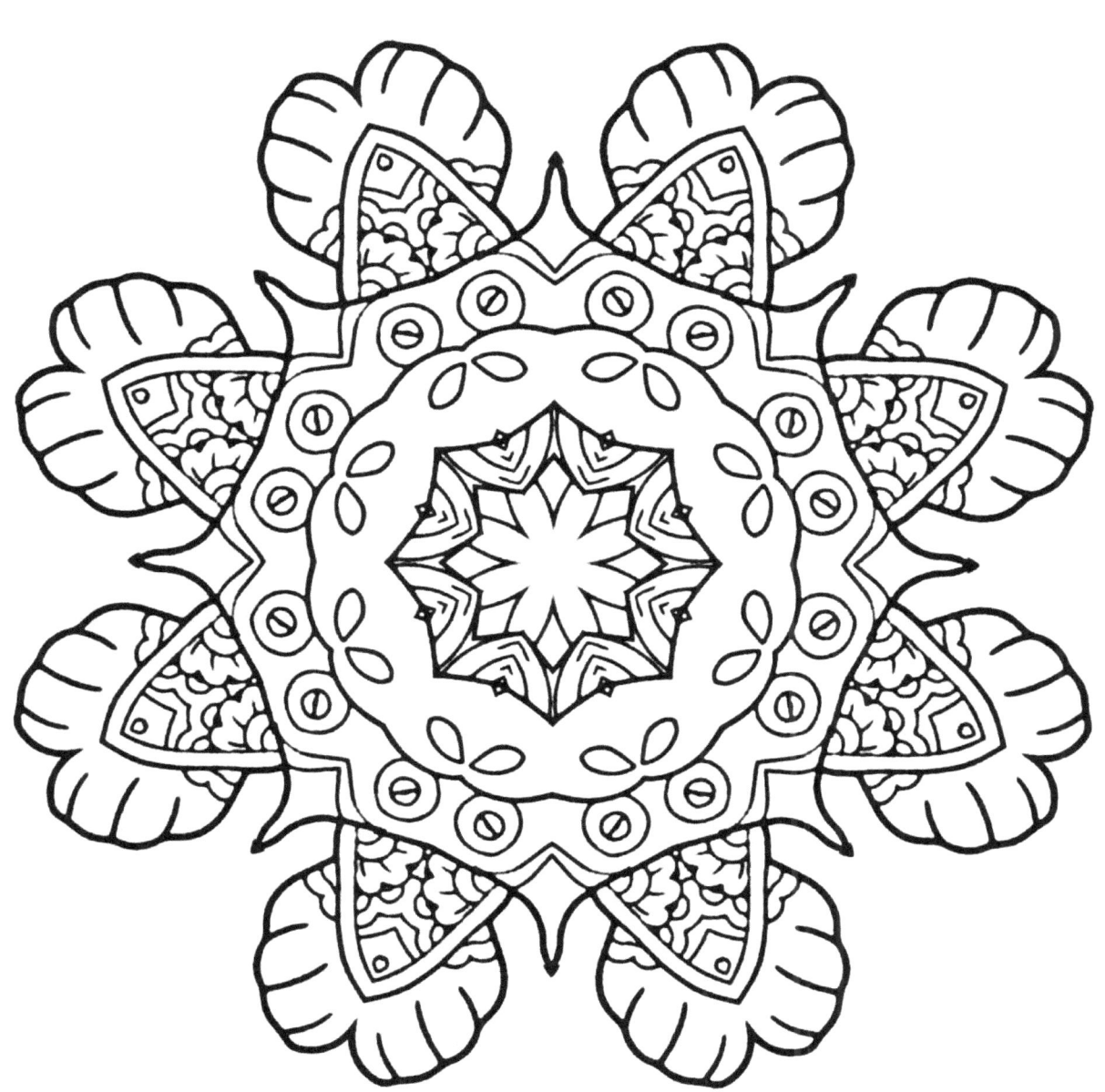

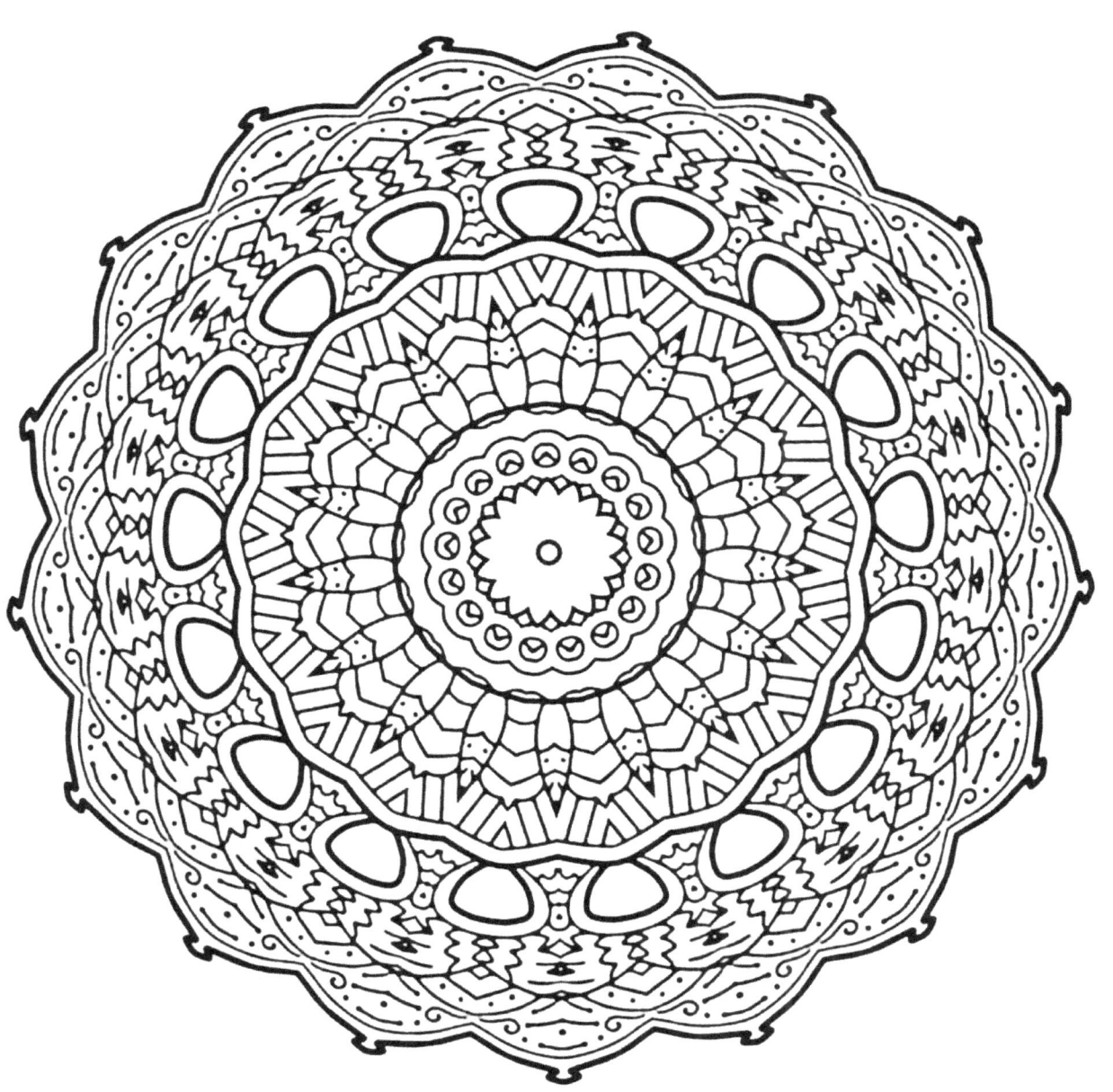

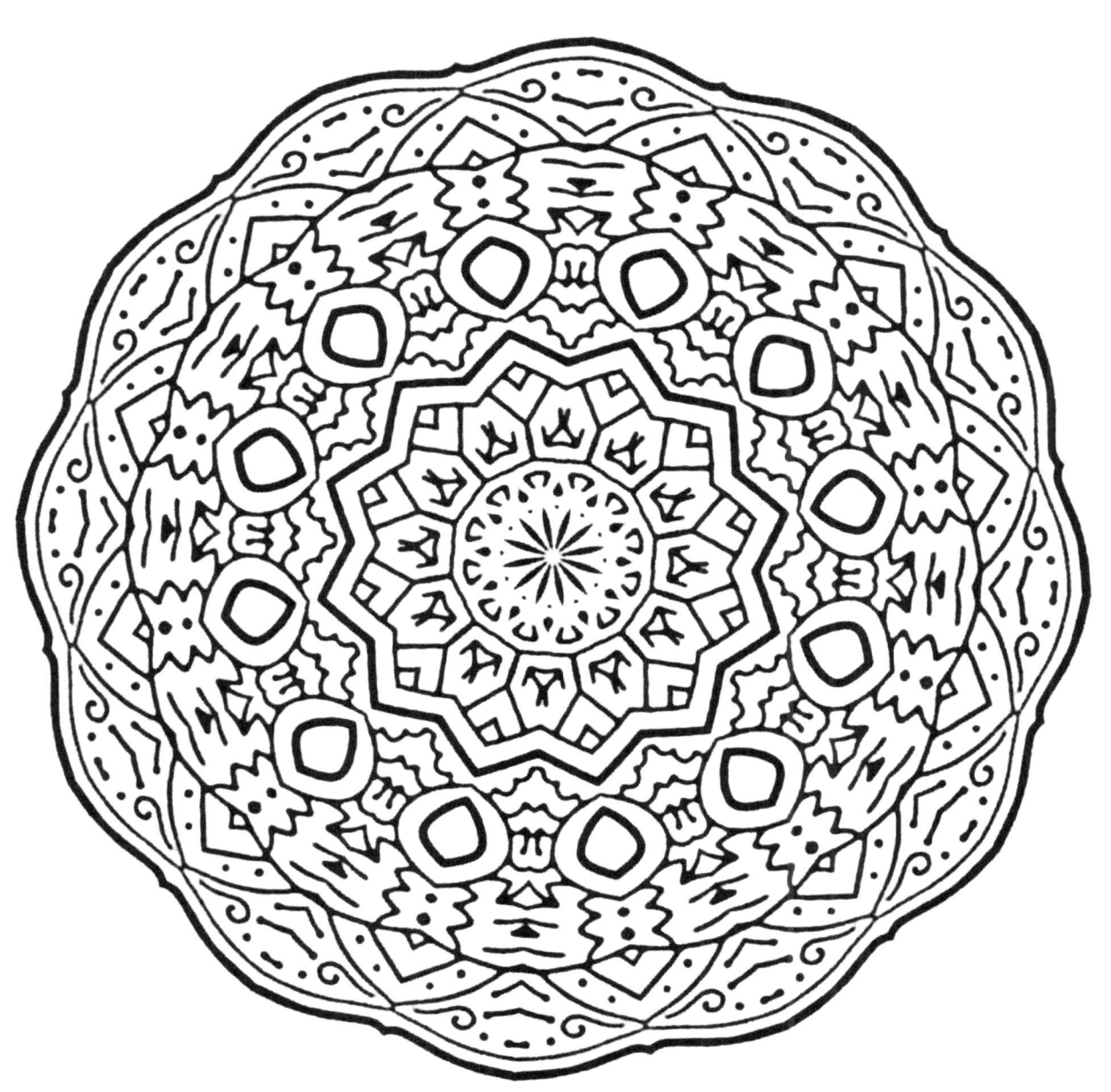

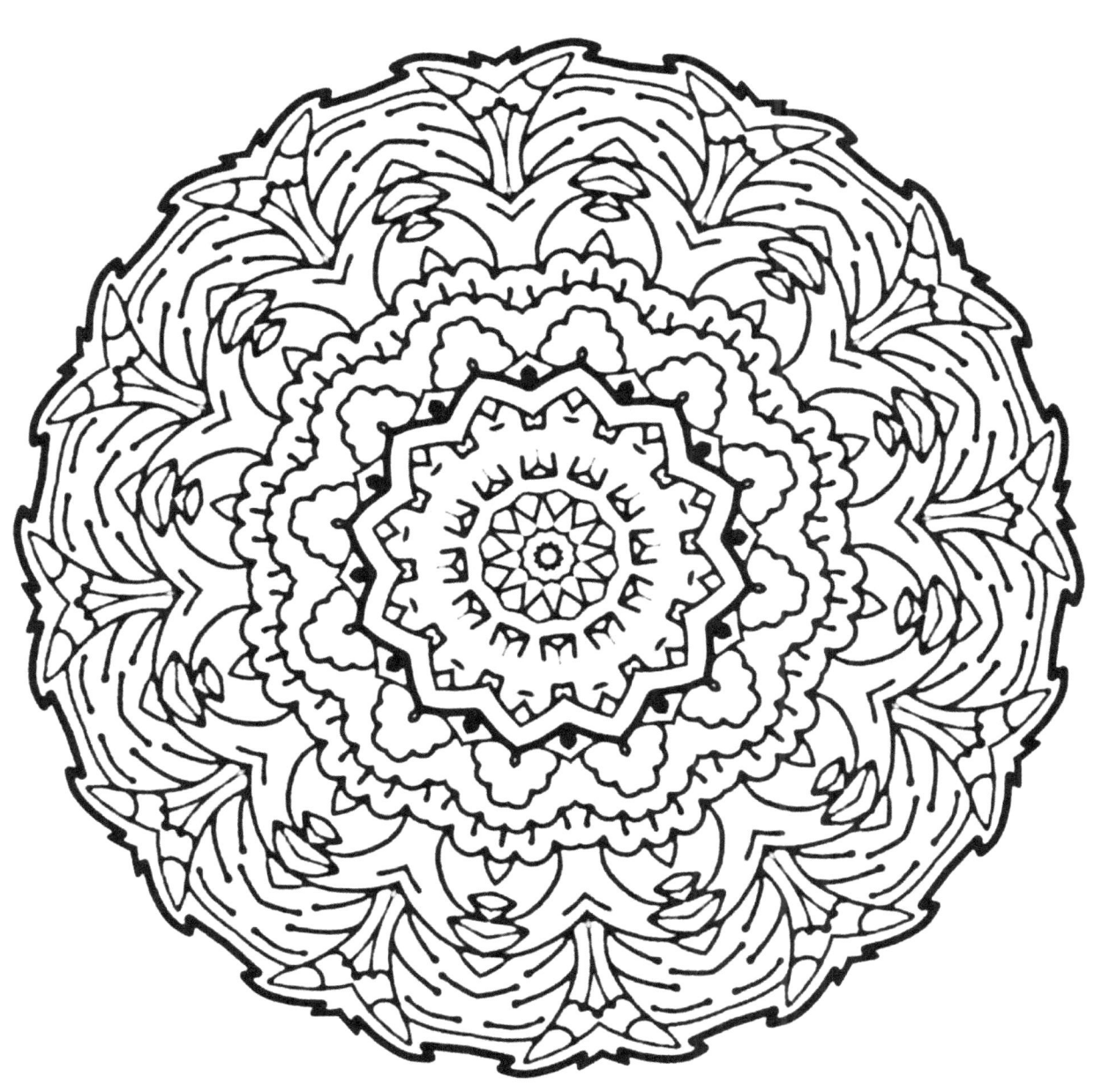

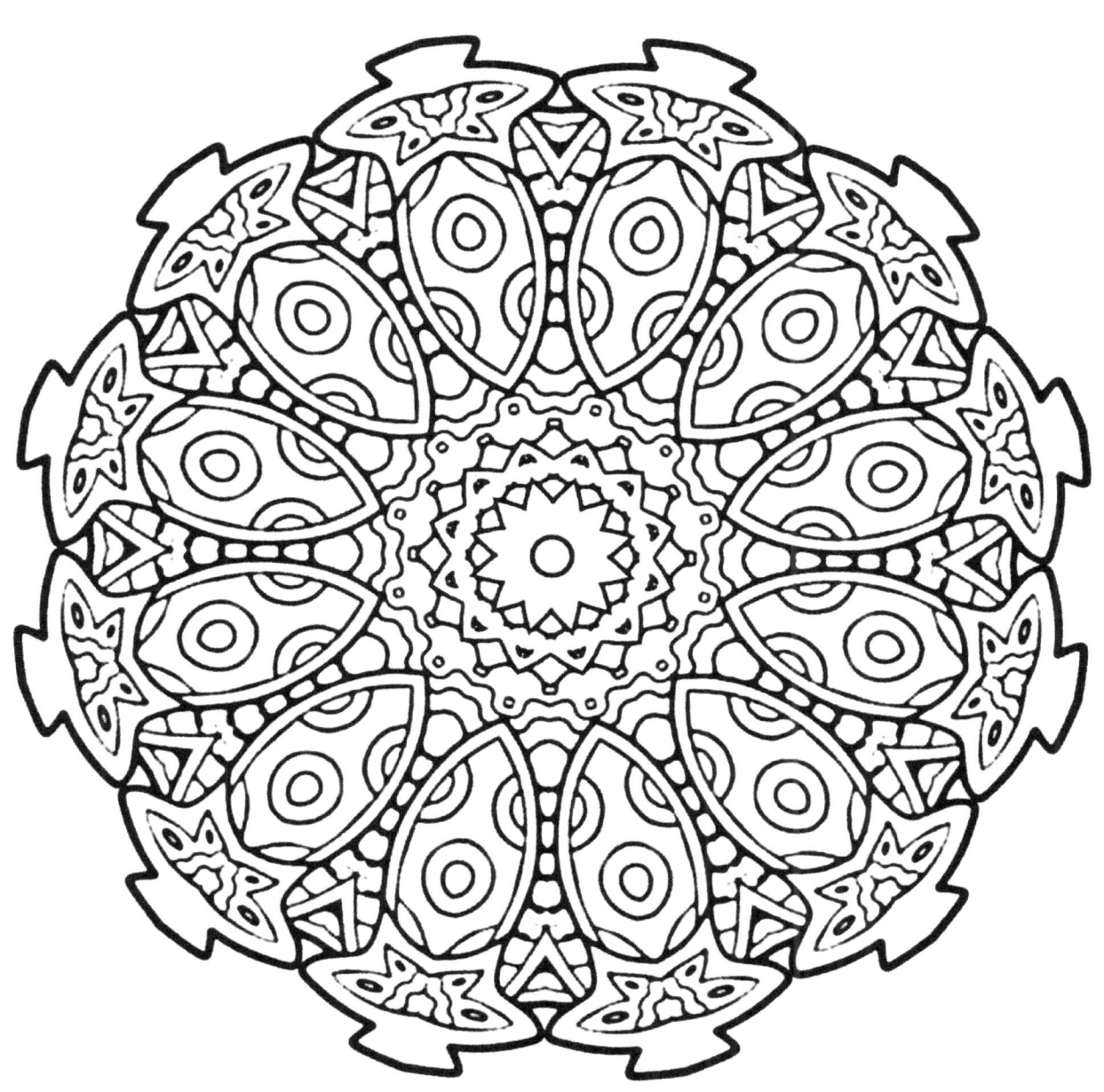

Thank you

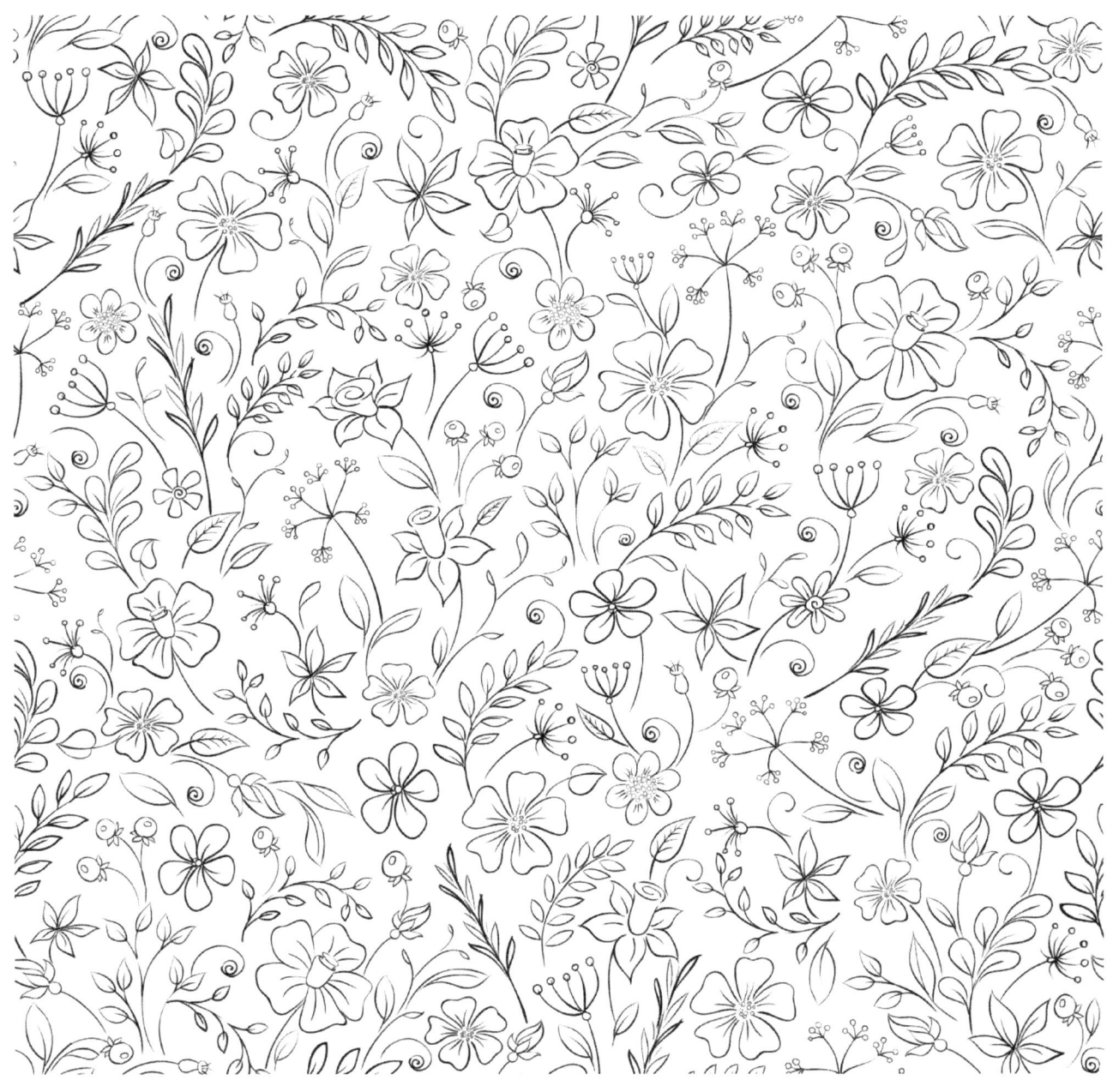

www.ingramcontent.com/pod-product-compliance
Lightning Source LLC
Chambersburg PA
CBHW081741170526
45167CB00009B/3902